Customer's objections are **NOT** "No"

Closing Sales

How to Handle Common Customers' Objections

Majority of customers could have bought products they ask for if sales people could be able to handle common objections.

Salehe A Nantembelele

Published by:

Create Space Independent Publishing Platform

United State of America

Copyright © 2016 Create Space Independent Publishing Platform
All rights reserved.

ISBN-13: 978-1539175780

ISBN-10: 1539175782

This page intentionally left blank

To three women I love the most:

Anne, Rukia & Fatuma

Table of Content

Introduction _____ 6

What are objections? _____ 7

How should you handle objections? _____ 8

1) 1, 2, 3 Close (Triple Hammer Strike Close) _____ 9

2) The Affordability Close _____ 10

3) The Alternative Choice Close _____ 12

4) The Apology Close _____ 13

5) The Artisan Close _____ 14

6) The Ask the Manager Close _____ 16

7) The Assumptive Close _____ 18

8) The Benjamin Franklin Close (Balance Sheet Close) __ 20

9) Best Time Close (Be Back Close) _____ 22

10) Feasible Flexible Close _____ 24

11) Feel, Felt, Found Close _____ 25

12) Freebie or Bonus Close _____ 27

About the Author _____ 28

Introduction

It is true that customers usually ask for the products with the intention of purchasing or get the information that will help them to be prepared to buy. Very few times customers just ask for a product for other reasons.

Based on the above truth, assuming other factor remain constant, for most customers who visit your show room or shop should buy or coming back to buy in few days to few months.

But why there is a large number of customers who shows intention but at the end of the day they end up not buying the product? There are several reasons but most of them is **the way we close our sales.**

In this book we have analized common objections/rejections raised by customers and how to handle them and turn your **"leaving cutomer"** to **"buying customer"**.

The book is designed to be short, clear, to the point and use actual phrases as examples that you may use when closing sales with objecting customer.

Now let see what is objection in short as we define it and start learning different types of objections.

What are objections?

Objections are quite literally another way for the customer to tell you that they do not understand, that they need more details, or that they are confused.

An objection is not a "NO", a "NO" is a "No". If a customer was not interested in your product he would not even bother making an objection, he would just say "No thank you".

Many sales people see an objection as a show stopper, they are wrong. When an objection is raised, the sales person's job has just started. If every customer bought a product without objections, sales people would be replaced with order takers – trained monkeys even.

If you find that you are facing a lot of objections, then there may be an issue – possibly with you. Perhaps it is your persona, your body language, your approach, the way you meet and greet customers. If you are unsure, speak to your peers, or your manager to discuss together and find out why that is happening.

Now hang on, look at the list of objections, pick out the one that keeps coming up and try the approach we show you. And, fingers crossed, whatch your closing ration increase.

How should you handle objections?

In the old days we used to ignore them, however these days... customers know and they will hold it against you for the whole transaction - perhaps making up objections just to make you work harder for the deal.

E ... Empathise:	"I can understand that" "I'm glad you brought that up" "Many of my customers..."
M.... Mirror Back:	"So what you're saying is..."
P.... Permission:	"Can I ask you a question?"
A.... Ask the question:	"What is it specifically...?" "Suppose that wasn't an issue"
T.... Take the Time to clarify:	"So, just to clarify my thinking, is this the only concern you have?
H.... Help them own it	"So if I could get my manager to... you would...?"
Y.... Get the YES	"Ok, that's great! Let me grab your autograph here to ok the go ahead/commit to the offer/submit the offer"

1) 1, 2, 3 Close (Triple Hammer Strike Close)

This close should be used regularly by all sales people as it outlines 3 positive points in the sales process, presentation or negotiation.

Some frequently used examples are:

- ✓ "The great thing about the SS-V is that it gives you 6.0L engine which means you also get (1) 260kW of power, (2) Active Fuel Management and (3) 6 speed Automatic Transmission with Active Select."
- ✓ "The official offer gives you the (1) 5 Yr Warranty, (2) 3 Yrs Roadside Assistance and (3) 3 years capped servicing costs."
- ✓ "If we can get a deal done now, my manager has guaranteed he will give you yesterdays sale offer - (1) Headlamp protectors, (2) Full tank of Fuel, and (3) Tailored Floor Mats"

Hopefully you see how the 3 items mentioned in one swift fluid statement reinforces the impact of value, allowing minimum time to counter with a negative retort. Even if the customer comes back with "...and what about Weather shields" you can state that you are already giving him/her 3 free items and reply with "Well, which would you like to exchange for the weather shields?"

As stated, use this technique often.

2) The Affordability Close

Every week we hear people say "I can't afford it" or "I don't know if it is worth it". This can easily be overcome providing the customer trusts you, a business manager (BM/Finance Manager/F and I) and the objection is not a real objection.

There are a couple of ways to handle this:

- ✓ Many dealerships feel very strongly that customers should be introduced to the business manager well before negotiation stage. We would recommend prior to the test drive, and maybe even before the vehicle selection stage. Refer to the section on Introduction to Finance for recommended techniques. The BM will then break down the initial "Big Price" to bite sized monthly payments, after using a "Capacity Test" on the customer.
- ✓ Always ask the customer how much they were looking to invest per month
- ✓ Find a way to show value, e.g. LPG or Diesel "While the initial investment may seem higher than conventional fueled vehicles, based upon the KM's you do, you will recoup the costs rather quickly, perhaps in a year, and at that point start to enjoy fuel savings"
- ✓ Outline Capped servicing costs, therefore promoting "savings" throughout the ownership

- ✓ Also, a very important approach would be to outline the cost of not upgrading to your vehicle, e.g. driving an old model constantly in need of maintenance VS your new, capped price serviced, fuel efficient model.
- ✓ Use the "reduce to the ridiculous" Close
- ✓ "If we are able to reduce the price closer to the amount you are indicating, would be able to place your order now?"

This type of close works well for people who are using "I can't afford it" as an excuse, as you are showing them affordability at a level they can't deny. If they used the objection as a simple excuse, then they will either agree and buy or jump to another Excuse/Objection.

If it was a real objection, then it will be obvious and you can gracefully back out of the negotiation stage or switch them to an appropriate vehicle.

Remember:
- ✓ Always live by the law of attraction. Your actions will always attract a reaction.
- ✓ Do not sign people up for a vehicle that they honestly can not afford - your career will plummet from these negative actions.

3) The Alternative Choice Close

This close is a cousin to the Assumptive close and it works by offering more than one clearly defined alternative to the customer. The catch is too many alternatives will cause the customer to become confused and perhaps vacillate.

- ✓ Now, I know you wanted black, and we can deliver black to you within 120 days. Now if you wanted something sooner, we can have Red prepared for your pickup within a week
- ✓ I understand that you requested Automatic in Red, however we only have a Manual in Red, or...an Automatic in Silver.
- ✓ (Assume) Would you like the car ready for pickup on Thursday, or can you wait till Saturday?
- ✓ (Assume) Would you like me to arrange for the Generic Number Plates, or would you prefer to pick your own?

When used correctly, this close will take the stressful large decision away from the customer and their focus will be on the smaller decision, relaxing their posture towards you and making the process seamless.

4) The Apology Close

The Apology close, is where the salesperson apologises for not yet helping the customer purchase. It states that the customer knows that the car is perfect for them, and the price is right, but they still have not bought - so it must be the sales persons fault for missing something in the explanation and making it obvious that the next step is to place the order.

> "I owe you an apology. Somewhere along the line, I must have left out important information, or in some way left you room for doubt. We both know this product suits your needs perfectly, and so the fault here must be with me".

It is funny that a statement where you absorb the blame for the customers hesitation works so well.

Why does it work? It takes the blame off the customer and they will usually say "no, no it's not you it's...." the real objection.

5) The Artisan Close

This is where you, as the sales person outline the incredible engineering, talent, design skill, modernisation that has gone into the the vehicle you are promoting - **you are building value!**

If a customer thinks that a vehicle is cheaply built, either because of the old design, or the "cheap" plastics, or the simply "shocking" presentation by the salesperson, the customer can not be expected to pay the price being asked.

So, if you are asking $1.7 Million for the Bugatti Veyron, you would be emphasising the 5 week build, the extreme research that goes into the designing, the fact that all parts are bubble wrapped and fitted by hand.

If you were selling a Corolla (just an example, don't be offended if you sell Toyota), you would not emphasise the few hours it takes to build, however you would sell the concept of "Toyota's perceived reliability", the modern design, the months of testing that went into making sure the interior was suitable for most drivers, etc.

A perfect example that comes to mind was Daewoo selling their vehicles as Italian designed - which they were, for Pininfarina was their design team for some of their models.

Let's see some examples:

- ✓ I know you may think the Gearshifter being in that position seems like a small thing, but it took months of gathering feedback to find the optimal position
- ✓ Now while steering seems such a trivial thing, the Electronic Steering Assist program we use has taken years to get to such a perfect design.
- ✓ The suspension used in this particular model is the exact same suspension used in our Racing model!

Remember, the Artisan Close can be used to sell your business, the services provided, the many years that you and your company have supported the local community, and so on. Think outside the square - but always remain honest.

6) The Ask the Manager Close

Now, this close should always be used - even if you are a manager or senior salesperson. If the customer thinks you have control of the prices, they will ask you personally for everything under the sun, and will not recognise when the "Bottom Dollar" IS the bottom dollar.

The close goes along these lines:

"I am unsure if the price you are proposing is feasible, however should I be able to get the manager to agree to a price close to what you are proposing, would you reserve the right to change your mind and place an order?"

"I have not seen anyone achieve that sort of discount/inclusion in the past, however IF by some chance the manager decides that it is acceptable to give you what you propose, how much deposit can I tell him/her you will leave?"

As you can see, the decision is taken away from you, and placed upon your manager, or someone appearing to be a manager. Customers also appreciate this close for it means that you have given them everything you possible could and now "important" people will be involved in their transaction.

Have you ever noticed that after much time negotiating with the customers, the sales person seems exasperated, only to have another peer/manager step in and instantly close the deal using the same details that the salesperson had been using for the last half hour?

Sometimes customers just want another person or manager involved - it is selfish of the customer, but it makes things easy for salespeople who know of it

HINT:

Have fun with this close. Use wild "loud" gestures when talking to the manager, showing the customer how many energy you are putting in for them. When the customer sees you commit so much to the manager, they will feel that they must commit to YOU - by buying the product, and mostly with a much smaller discount than initially proposed.

7) The Assumptive Close

Statistics have shown that up to 85% of the people walking into your Dealership made a decision to buy a vehicle before they even walked out their front door. Further reports also state that 81% of the people that come into your dealership buy a vehicle within 7 days of starting their shopping around. Why would you want to know this? Because it quite simply proves that a majority of the customers you talk talk to are in reality - buyers.

Many customers have learned from earlier poor experiences to hide their interest in purchasing, masking their zeal and excitement.

Of course, every Salesperson knows to trial close, and if the trial closes gain positive responses from the customer, then the following close is perfect for you to use. Remain confident, have a strong posture and "assume" they are ready to buy. Take your clients inside, sit them down, and take out your company paperwork/start up your purchasing software. Do not talk yet, do not act nervously.

"Mr and Mrs Jones, do you want new Number plates or are we using plates you have have on hold/from your trade in? And your current address is....? Ok, and your home phone number...? Mobile number? Work number? And you wanted the manual in red."

Use the numbers that you have previously discussed on the paperwork, and if no discussion has been held, use the RRP.

"Ok, so that is sorted, I will just grab it off the printer. Ok now, lets clarify that I have got all your details correct, and you can see the vehicle details here, with the changeover price here, and as discussed we should have it ready for delivery by (accurate date). All we need now is your autograph here, and I will pop it in for my manager to sign off as well. Congratulations! How easy was that?"

Now, some times you may have a customer decline from signing as they "never sign their first offer". This is where the **"feel, felt, found close"** can be used.

8) The Benjamin Franklin Close (Balance Sheet Close)

The Benjamin Franklin Close, also called the Balance Sheet close, is where the salesperson and the prospect build together a pros-and-cons list of whether to buy the product, with the salesperson trying to ensure the pros list is longer than the cons.

Let's use the example below, with Pro's on the left and Con's on the right, noticing that the sales person would obviously want to point out many more Pro's and let the customer come up with the Con's themselves.

Great Steering	6 speed Auto, instead of 7
Sunroof	No Sat Nav
20 inch Alloys	No DRL's
Body Kit	
Leather Trim	
Quad Exhaust	
HUD	
Adaptive Cruise control	

And remember, make it look like the customer is creating the list, but if you see the Con's catching up on the Pro's, "remind" them of a positive.

9) Best Time Close (Be Back Close)

How many times have you had a customer say, "I will be back". Now for Arnie, that is a great phrase and we believe him, but for customers, we all know it is usually a line. How do we get around this line?

One way is by using the "Best Time Close", where the salesperson quite simply states why "now" is a much beneficial time to place an order than when the customer "comes back". Reasons to place an order now could include any of the following as well as many not mentioned:

- ✓ The sale ends at 5 O'clock and we don't know when this level of discount will be seen again
- ✓ The bonuses paid by the factory are only available on MY13 models, and we have....only 2 left. You should place your order now on one of these vehicles while they are still available. Being 2014 we won't see any NEW last years models.
- ✓ It is a Xmas sale, and Xmas is now over - we do not know when the sale will be cut off
- ✓ The boss is currently on leave and we have the 2IC running the show. NOW is the time to place an order as the 2IC will want to do as many deals as possible to impress management.

This close works by showing value in doing something NOW and building urgency - not by promoting procrastination.

10) Feasible Flexible Close

This close is in the toolbox of every successful salesperson out there. When you have a price haggler in front of you, on the phone, or via email, this close gets you closer where you want to be in the negotiation stage OR exposes the customer as not being genuine.

"Now, I really appreciate your offer as I know it is a genuine offer to purchase this vehicle, which suits all your needs. From my experience working with my manager and through many transactions around this type of car I don't know if it is gong to be feasible to get to the $ that you are requesting. If I can get my manager to be a little bit more flexible on the price they are offering you, could I expect you to be a little bit more flexible on the price you are proposing?"

Flexibility is contextual - it may be single dollars, hundreds of dollars or thousands. The main thing this close exposes is:

- ✓ Does the customer really want to co-operate?
- ✓ Is the customer stuck at one price or can they move a little?
- ✓ Are they just objecting to the price because they don;t know how to tell you they don't want it?

11) Feel, Felt, Found Close

This close can be used to handle almost any objection. The idea with any objection is not to make the customer feel like a freak or different to others. For e.g. Sales people should not say "oh, I have not heard that one before. I don't understand why that stops you from buying?" This will annihilate any rapport you have worked so hard to build and you might as well hand the customer to another salesperson.

The idea is to make the customer feel like their objection is understood, and reasonable. "I understand exactly how you FEEL" . By saying this you you are not challenging the objection, and therefore the customer, but instead you are empathising with them, reinforcing all the rapport you have already compiled with them.

The next step is to let the potential client know that other customers of yours FELT exactly the same. This makes the customer feel like they are in "well-known" waters and they "fit" in to a group of customers. It also states that other Customers had this same issue yet they still became Clients, and you will notice the customers barrier/wall will drop a little (or a lot).

The final step is to state that while your clients felt that way they FOUND that ......and this is where you insert a solution.

The solution may be along the lines of any topic. Some examples are below:

> "I understand how you FEEL. For many of my current clients FELT exactly the same way when they were given the option of red. However, what they FOUND was that the paint used in this day and age is much more resistant to the sun and therefore fades much less than in the past."

> "I understand how you FEEL, for many of my current clients FELT exactly the same way when they were told we no longer offer Manual Transmissions. What they FOUND though was that the Automatics offer much better acceleration, fuel efficiency and towing capacity, while also satisfying the need to shift gears with the Active Shift Mode."

As you can see from the examples, this close can be easily used and if you are prepared to think on your feet, you can overcome many objections by using it with the correct timing and posture.

12) Freebie or Bonus Close

Now, when a customer is vacillating and time is running short, sometimes the "Have to go home and think about it" objection is looming just around the corner. A great way to prevent this and close the deal is to offer a surprise freebie or "bonus" item.

The item should be something of use to the customer and also un-asked for by the customer. An example could be

"Now, I know that you love the car, and because you have been so patient with me, I am including a free set of mat for you because today has been such a great day, and I have really enjoyed dealing with you."

From this close, many deals can be made, providing that the customer sees integrity and a genuine generosity from the salesperson. The successful close may be because the customer feels they now "owe" the salesperson, or a sense of "something for nothing". For whatever reason, it works.

HINT:

The "freebie" is free to the customer - not to you or your dealership. This close does have an effect on your profit margin, so only offer if you have authorisation from management and ensure that the profit is sufficient enough to cover the "freebie".

About the Author

Salehe A Nantembelele has a good experience in business from doing business including online businesses in the past eight years. Currently he is a president of Yuu Company (group of four business units) and a sole owner of Tanzania Website Design (http://www.tanzaniawebsitedesign.com/).

Salehe A Nantembelele is a former Executive Accountant of Taris Consult (sister company of Health Focus Ltd) where he worked for two years and lead to tremendous improvement in the business operations of the group company.

He has a bachelor of commerce (B.com) specialized in accounting taken from University of Dar Es Salaam Business School (UDBS), Currently He is on the way to pursue Master in Business Administration (MBA).

Salehe A Nantembelele is good speaker with rich contents in enterpreneurship, business and blogging in general. He mostly present in various seminars that he is invited.

Salehe A Nantembelele is in love with Amne S Issa – a girl he married in 2014.

www.ingramcontent.com/pod-product-compliance
Lightning Source LLC
Chambersburg PA
CBHW071834200526
45169CB00018B/1505